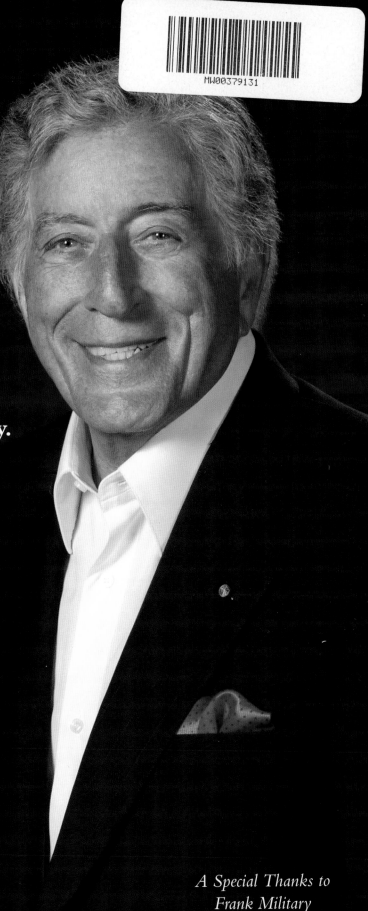

Tony Bennett

Duets
An American Classic

Arranged by Dan Coates

**It's Tony Bennett's 80th birthday.
And look who's coming to the party.**

Bono

Michael Bublé

Elvis Costello

Celine Dion

Dixie Chicks

Billy Joel

Elton John

Juanes

Diana Krall

k.d. lang

John Legend

Paul McCartney

Tim McGraw

George Michael

Sting

Barbra Streisand

James Taylor

Stevie Wonder

*A Special Thanks to
Frank Military*

Art Direction and Design: Josh Cheuse
Photography: Paul Drinkwater / NBC
Cover Album Art: Ian Wright

Mosaic based on a photograph by Mark Seliger.
Photos courtesy of: SONY BMG Archives, Photofest, Everett Collection,
Michael Ochs Archives, Retna and The Bennett Family Collection

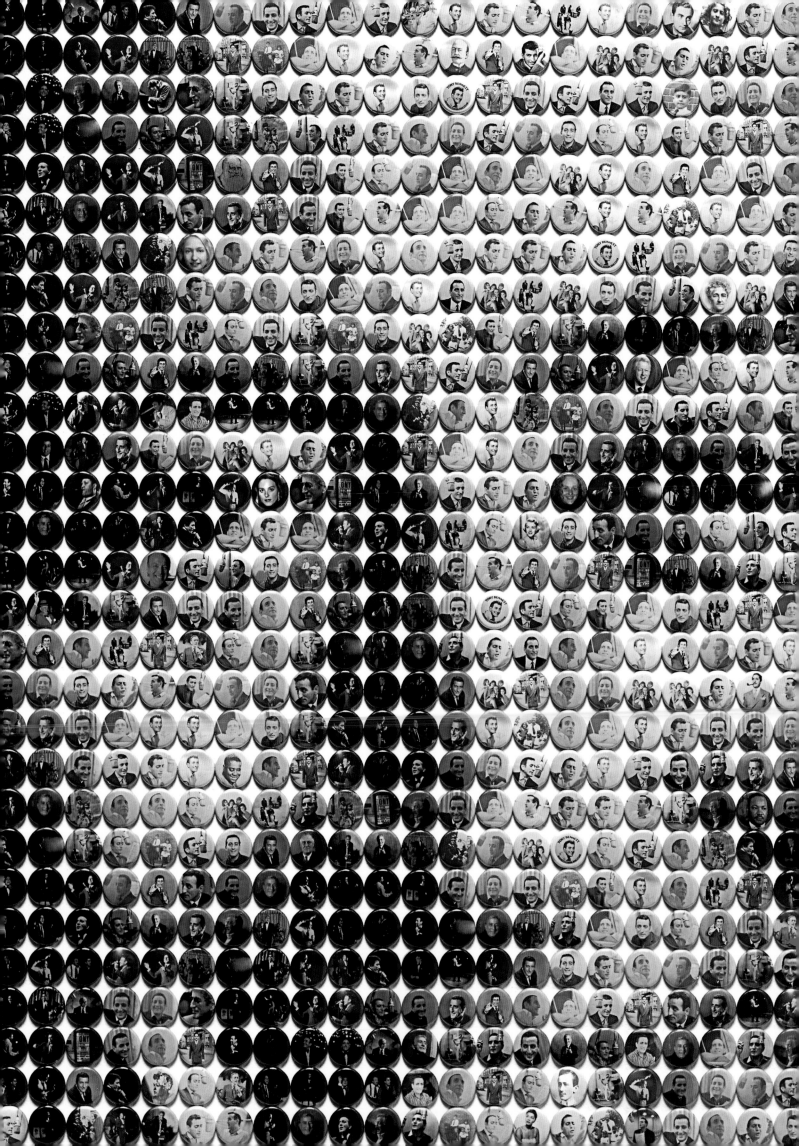

CONTENTS

VOLUME #

14 **ARE YOU HAVIN' ANY FUN?**
with Elvis Costello

1 11 **BECAUSE OF YOU**
with k.d. lang

2 18 **THE BEST IS YET TO COME**
with Diana Krall

1 23 **THE BOULEVARD OF BROKEN DREAMS**
with Sting

4 26 **COLD, COLD HEART**
with Tim McGraw

4 29 **FOR ONCE IN MY LIFE**
with Stevie Wonder

2 32 **THE GOOD LIFE**
with Billy Joel

4 38 **HOW DO YOU KEEP THE MUSIC PLAYING?**
with George Michael

2 35 **I LEFT MY HEART IN SAN FRANCISCO**

2 42 **I WANNA BE AROUND**
with Bono

3 45 **IF I RULED THE WORLD**
with Celine Dion

1 48 **JUST IN TIME**
with Michael Bublé

1 51 **LULLABY OF BROADWAY**
with the Dixie Chicks

2 54 **PUT ON A HAPPY FACE**
with James Taylor

1 60 **RAGS TO RICHES**
with Elton John

3 57 **THE SHADOW OF YOUR SMILE**
with Juanes

62 **SING, YOU SINNERS**
with John Legend

3 66 **SMILE**
with Barbra Streisand

3 69 **THE VERY THOUGHT OF YOU**
with Paul McCartney

Tony Bennett

Duets – An American Classic

(RPM Records/Columbia Records)

Tony Bennett turns 80 this year and amidst the tributes, honors and accolades, the world's most down-to-earth living legend is celebrating this milestone the same way he essentially lives his life: enjoying each moment to the fullest, weathering the storms with good cheer and optimism, and connecting to people everywhere through the magic of his music and the power of his art.

"Mr. Bennett," wrote Stephen Holden in The New York Times (August 2, 2006), "has steadfastly remained the embodiment of heart in popular music. He pours it into every note he sings and every phrase he swings with a sophistication that deepens his unguarded emotional directness. In the polluted sea of irony, bad faith and grotesque attitudinizing that pop music has become, he is a rock of integrity."

As he has done virtually every year or so since the 1950s, the forever young octogenarian has recorded a new album, an unaffected and unabashed exaltation of what he calls "the Great American Songbook," a timeless treasure trove of standards, classics, and sometimes overlooked gems of traditional pop and swinging jazz.

This year's Tony Bennett album, *Duets – An American Classic* (the artist's 13th new studio collection since returning to Columbia Records two decades ago), finds the maestro reprising some of the best-loved songs in his repertoire as duets performed with some of the top names in contemporary music: Bono, Michael Bublé, Elvis Costello, Celine Dion, Dixie Chicks, Juanes, Billy Joel, Diana Krall, k.d. lang, John Legend, Paul McCartney, Tim McGraw, George Michael, Sting, Barbra Streisand, James Taylor and Stevie Wonder. Instrumental musical guests on Tony's *Duets – An American Classic* include trumpeter Chris Botti and violinist Pinchas Zukerman.

Tony recorded this landmark album in three locations in early 2006: Capitol Studios in Los Angeles; Bennett Studios in Englewood, New Jersey; and Abbey Road Studios in London. Producer Phil Ramone supervised the sessions, which, in keeping with a longstanding Bennett tradition, were recorded live, with each guest artist performing side-by-side with Tony. Tony's touring quartet—Lee Musiker on piano, Gray Sargent on guitar, Paul Langosch on bass and Harold Jones on drums—provided the basic accompaniments.

Tony's sons helped out with *Duets – An American Classic*, making the album a Bennett family affair. The record was recorded and mixed by Dae Bennett at Dae's Bennett Studios in Englewood, New Jersey and executive produced by Danny Bennett, who's served as Tony's manager for more than two decades.

With a set list of songs lovingly selected from the innumerable high points of Tony's six decades as a recording legend, *Duets – An American Classic* is a fitting crescendo to a career that only grows stronger with time.

"They were all rather quick," said Tony of the *Duets* sessions, "but one that knocked me out was the Dixie Chicks. They told me they'd never done anything like this before." Tony was referring to his duet with the Dixie Chicks on the album's opening track, "Lullaby of Broadway." (The Harry Warren-Al Dubin composition from the Busby Berkeley film, "Gold Diggers of 1935," had been a highlight of his 1957 album, *The Beat of My Heart*, a conceptual masterpiece which showcased drumming by legends like Art Blakey, Jo Jones, Chico Hamilton, and Sabu and established Tony Bennett as a premier jazz vocalist.)

"Smile," Tony's duet with Barbra Streisand, also has cinematic overtones, having been penned by Charlie Chaplin for his classic 1936 film "Modern Times." "This was a bull's-eye as far as I'm concerned," Tony commented on Streisand's performance. "She's always good, but this sounded to me like a homerun in the way our voices blended. And what I like about

'Smile' is that it's timeless. 'Smile' is what it's all about: 'You find life is still worthwhile, if you just smile.'" (Bennett had a hit single with a solo version of "Smile" in 1959.)

Tony's outlook on life resonates in "Put On a Happy Face," his duet with James Taylor.

"Part of my personal philosophy as an entertainer is to stay optimistic about things, that there's a light at the end of the tunnel no matter how bleak things get," says Tony. "What I like about what happened with James Taylor is that I never knew that he was such a great improviser. He's a natural—as good as any jazz soloist I've ever heard. He's very spontaneous and never sings the same way twice, and there's always a new thought coming into his mind. There's a nice, natural way about him, and he's so intelligent." (Tony previously recorded "Put On A Happy Face," a song from the 1960s musical "Bye Bye Birdie," as a duet with Rosie O'Donnell for his 1998 album *The Playground*.)

Bennett paired off with Paul McCartney on the incomparable standard, "The Very Thought of You," penned by the British composer/bandleader Ray Noble. "Ray also wrote the big swing tune 'Cherokee' and was the equivalent in England to Cole Porter," said Bennett. "'The Very Thought of You' is a gorgeous song that Paul specifically wanted to do with me— and it was a knockout doing it with him. We did it at Abbey Road, so right away he got very nostalgic telling me where John and the rest of them stood when they recorded there. When I first came to Britain, I was at Wembley Stadium and they told me to give some awards to some new artists—two big groups. One was the Beatles and one was the Rolling Stones, so I gave them their first music awards. And when I looked at the Beatles—who were just getting popular—I looked at the guy in the middle and felt instinctively that he was going to make it because he had that look and spirit about him, and it was Paul. And I still feel that way—it was very easy to sing with him."

Tony revisited his 1965 hit, "The Shadow of Your Smile," as a duet with the Latin crossover sensation Juanes. "To me, Johnny Mandel is just the best composer of contemporary music that I know of," said Bennett of the song's composer (Paul Francis Webster penned the lyrics). "'Emily' and 'A Time for Love' are beautiful songs that will eventually go into the American Songbook like those of Gershwin and Porter. But what I had fun with was Juanes. He's one of the nicest performers I've ever met. I had to sing Spanish phonetically with him, and he helped me so much to make sure I got the right pronunciation."

For their track on **Duets – An American Classic**, Tony Bennett and Elton John re-recorded Tony's smash single, "Rags to Riches," which held down the #1 spot on America's charts for eight weeks in 1953. (Tony's solo version may be heard in the soundtrack to Martin Scorsese's 1990 film, "Goodfellas.") "Elton sat down at the piano after saying hello, then played the whole thing and said, 'Let's do it,'" Tony observed, "and it was done in three takes."

Piano man Billy Joel proved equally at ease working with Bennett on a new version of "The Good Life," a huge hit for Bennett in 1963. Working with Joel, said Bennett, "was terrific. I like Billy personally, we get along great, and I consider him a major talent. He's just a natural, and he knew exactly what to do."

Tony returned to one of his very first hits, his pop version of Hank Williams' "Cold, Cold Heart," for his duet with contemporary country star Tim McGraw. "The song's a masterpiece," affirmed Bennett, who, to this day, revels in retelling how Hank Williams actually called him in 1951— when Tony's cover version was in the middle of its six week run at #1—and told him, "Thanks for ruining my song." "The two immortals in my mind are Billie Holiday, from Harlem, and Hank Williams, from the South," Bennett continues. He points out that his link with the country music crowd was recently refreshed when Tim McGraw introduced him in the audience at his concert at Madison Square Garden. "The place went crazy," Tony laughs, "but Tim's a great guy. He's very authentic, and he sang just wonderfully—and we had a lot of laughs."

Tony Bennett and Diana Krall teamed on a new interpretation of "The Best Is Yet To Come," Cy Coleman and Carolyn Leigh composition which Bennett turned into an enduring standard via his 1962 album, *I Left My Heart In San Francisco*. "Diana's a great jazz singer, and her piano playing gets better and better every year," says Tony. "She just sat down at the piano and played, and it was just so natural and perfect and there was a lot of ad-libbing and it ended up being a joy."

Many of the songs on **Duets – An American Classic** were first introduced to the public by Tony Bennett. In fact, Tony had experienced some chart success with his 1967 version of "For Once In My Life" more than a year before Stevie Wonder made it one of his signature songs. Tony and Stevie perform it together on **Duets – An American Classic**. "Ron Miller—a very nice guy—composed it," Bennett recalls. "I was at a supper club in Detroit—The Rooster Tail—and Ron said, 'I have a song you might like.' I heard it and said that I'd love to record it and he was thrilled. Then Stevie, who was still very young, put a beat behind it when Motown was coming into its own and he sold millions. So this is such a wonderful thing that we both recorded it together. Stevie slipped in three notes of 'I Left My Heart in San Francisco' into his harmonica solo and we all got a laugh. I consider Stevie Wonder one of the great jazz artists of all time—and such a thoughtful, beautiful human being." (Tony and Stevie worked together on "Everyday (I Have The Blues)," a track on Bennett's 2002 Grammy-winning album *Playin' with My Friends: Bennett Sings the Blues*".)

Elvis Costello, who contributed to Tony's 1994 Grammy-winning Album of the Year, *MTV Unplugged*, collaborates on "Are You Havin' Any Fun?," a song that first appeared on 1958's groundbreaking *Basie Swings, Bennett Sings*. Tony Bennett was the first male pop star to sing with Count Basie. "Elvis just went in," says Tony, "and we did it and it came out just right."

k.d. lang, one of Tony Bennett's favorite singing partners, and jazz trumpeter Chris Botti join the master on a new version of his 1951 breakout smash, "Because of You," which spent 10 weeks at #1 and established Tony as one of the nation's most popular male vocalists. k.d. performed with Tony on his Grammy-winning *MTV Unplugged* and cut a Grammy-winning album with him, *A Wonderful World*, 2002. "She did it so relaxed—and with so much feeling," Tony reveals, "and Chris played beautifully."

Contemporary crooner Michael Bublé was enlisted to team with Bennett for the **Duets** recording of his 1956 hit "Just in Time," a Betty Comden-Adolph Green-Jule Styne composition from "Bells Are Ringing," one of the many Broadway classics that have been introduced by Bennett. "I have a lot of faith in Michael," said Tony of the rising young pop vocalist. "He's like a performer from the old school—very smart, very intelligent."

One of Tony's very first singles, the regional hit "Boulevard of Broken Dreams" from 1950, has been recast in 2006 as a duet with Sting. "It was the first record I made on Columbia after [legendary A&R executive] Mitch Miller heard my demo and signed me up at the same time as Rosemary Clooney," Tony remembers with a smile. "We were the first American Idols. What happened with Sting—and what I hope for with any duet—is to be different. Our voices are different, and it's that contrast that makes for a good duet. The perfect example is Ella [Fitzgerald] with Louis Armstrong—gruff with sweet. What I love about is Sting is right away you know if I'm singing or Sting is because of the contrast, and that's what I wanted to get on all the duets. And I loved his interpretation:

It's completely different than the way I'm singing, and that difference makes for a good duet."

Bennett teamed up with another U.K. superstar, Bono, for the update of his Top 20 1963 hit "I Wanna Be Around." "Bono is different, too," he said. "He's such an international artist because of the politics."

Representing a new generation of recording artists, John Legend joined Bennett on "Sing You Sinners," one of the songs included in Bennett's historic 1962 *At Carnegie Hall* concert album. "I think he'll cross all the lines," Bennett predicted, sensing Legend's potential for film stardom as well as his already established stature as a Grammy-winning singer-songwriter. "He's a great composer, and a very relaxed performer."

For **Duets**, Tony revisited his 1962 signature hit "I Left My Heart In San Francisco," which his longtime musical director/pianist Ralph Sharon had uncovered in a drawer before bringing it to a young Tony Bennett more than forty years ago—the rest being history. Taking over Sharon's role on the new recording is the young jazz piano lion Bill Charlap, "who I consider to be the next Bill Evans," opined Bennett.

The album fittingly includes "How Do You Keep The Music Playing," the poignant Alan Bergman/Marilyn Bergman/Michel Legrand standard which Tony traditionally uses to close his concerts. (The song was a centerpiece track on Tony's 1986 return-to-Columbia Records album, *Art Of Excellence*.) Tony joined forces with George Michael on this track. "He made a perfect recording," said Tony.

That simple observation sums up the artistry of **Duets – An American Classic.**

"The artists all loved the way we recorded, and many said they'd like to record the way I do," said Bennett. "They didn't realize the amount of preparation that goes into it, and were surprised at the way we recorded live with just my original quartet." This, of course, is the way that Tony Bennett has always made his records.

Tony Bennett is an artist who moves the hearts and touches the souls of audiences. He's the singer's singer and has received high praise from his colleagues through the years, including Frank Sinatra who stated unequivocally, "Tony Bennett is the best singer in the business." He is an international treasure who was honored by the United Nations with their "Citizen of the World" award, which aptly describes the scope of his accomplishments.

The son of a grocer and Italian-born immigrant, Anthony Dominick Benedetto was born on August 3, 1926, in the Astoria section of Queens. He attended the High School of Industrial Arts in Manhattan, where he continued nurturing his two passions—singing and painting. His boyhood idols included Bing Crosby and Nat King Cole, both big influences on Bennett's easy, natural singing style. Tony sang while waiting tables as a teenager then performed with military bands during his Army enlistment in World War II. He later had vocal studies at the American Theatre Wing school. The first time Bennett sang in a nightclub was 1946 when he sat in with trombonist Tyree Glenn at the Shangri-La in Astoria.

Bennett's big break came in 1949 when comedian Bob Hope noticed him working with Pearl Bailey in Greenwich Village in New York City. As Bennett recalls, "Bob Hope came down to check out my act. He liked my singing so much that after the show he came back to see me in my dressing room and said, 'Come on kid, you're going to come to the Paramount and sing with me.' But first he told me he didn't care for my stage name (Joe Bari) and asked me what my real name was. I told him, 'My name is Anthony Dominick Benedetto,' and he said, 'We'll call you Tony Bennett.' And that's how it happened. A new Americanized name, the start of a wonderful career and a glorious adventure that has continued for fifty years."

With over 50 million records sold world-wide and platinum and gold albums to his credit, Bennett has received thirteen Grammy Awards and the Grammy Lifetime Achievement Award. The MTV generation first took Tony Bennett to heart during his appearance with the Red Hot Chili Peppers on the 1993 MTV Video Awards ceremony. He appeared on "MTV Unplugged" and the resulting recording of the same name garnered the singer Grammy's top award, "Album of the Year." "Tony Bennett has not just bridged the generation gap," pointed out The New York Times, "he has demolished it. He has solidly connected with a younger crowd weaned on rock. And there have been no compromises." Bennett credits his son and manager, Danny, for his success in capturing a whole new generation of listeners.

His initial successes came via a string of Columbia singles in the early 1950's, including such chart-toppers as "Because of You," "Rags To Riches" and a remake of Hank Williams' "Cold, Cold Heart." He had 24 songs in the Top 40, including "I Wanna Be Around," "The Good Life," "Who Can I Turn To (When Nobody Needs Me)" and his signature song, "I Left My Heart In San Francisco," which garnered him two Grammy Awards. Tony Bennett is one of a handful of artists to have new albums charting in the 50's, 60's, 70's, 80's, 90's

and beyond. He introduced a multitude of songs into the Great American Songbook that have since become standards for pop music. He has toured the world to sold out audiences with rave reviews whenever he performs. Bennett re-signed with Columbia Records in 1986 and released the critically acclaimed The Art Of Excellence. Since his 1991 show-stopping performance at the Grammy Awards of "When Do The Bells Ring For Me," from his Astoria album, he has received a string of Grammy Awards for releases including Steppin' Out, Perfectly Frank, and MTV Unplugged. In celebration of his unparalleled contributions to popular music with worldwide record sales of over 30 million, Columbia/Legacy assembled Forty Years: The Artistry Of Tony Bennett. The four-CD boxed set, released in 1991, chronicles the singer's stellar recording career and documents his growth as an artist inspiring Time magazine to call the collection "… the essence of why CD boxed sets are a blessing."

Tony Bennett became a Kennedy Center Honoree in 2005, was named an NEA Jazz Master in January of 2006, and has just been named this year's recipient of Billboard Magazine's prestigious Century Award, in honor of his outstanding contributions to music.

Tony Bennett has also received an Emmy Award and a Cable Ace Award for his groundbreaking television special, "Live By Request...Tony Bennett" which featured a unique interactive format in which the viewing audience called in song requests to the performer live during the program, a concept created by Bennett that has become a regular special on the A&E network. Bennett has also authored two books, What My Heart Has Seen, a beautifully bound edition of his paintings published in 1996, and The Good Life, his heartfelt autobiography released in 1998. He won his thirteenth Grammy Award in 2006 for The Art of Romance.

Tony Bennett is a dedicated painter whose interest in art began as a child. He continues to paint every day, even while touring internationally. He has exhibited his work in galleries around the world and he was chosen to be the official artist of the 2001 Kentucky Derby and created two original paintings celebrating this historic event. The United Nations has commissioned him for two paintings, including one for their 50th anniversary. His original painting "Homage to Hockney" is on permanent display at the Butler Institute of American Art and the landmark National Arts Club in New York is home to his painting, "Boy on Sailboat, Sydney Bay." Most recently his oil painting, entitled, "Central Park," was accepted to the Smithsonian's American Art Museum's permanent collection in Washington, DC.

Throughout his career, Tony Bennett has always put his heart and time into humanitarian concerns. He has raised millions of dollars for the Juvenile Diabetes Foundation which established a research fund in his name. His original paintings each year grace the cover of the American Cancer Society's annual holiday greeting card, proceeds from which are earmarked for cancer research. He is active in environmental concerns and has performed at fundraisers for both the Walden Woods Foundation and the Save the Rainforest Foundation. The Martin Luther King Center in Atlanta bestowed upon him their "Salute to Greatness Award" for his efforts to fight discrimination. He conceived and spearheaded the effort to honor his great friend with the establishment of the Frank Sinatra School of the Arts which opened its doors as a New York City public high school offering an extensive arts curriculum in September of 2001.

In the 1950's, thousands of screaming bobby-soxers surrounded the Paramount Theatre in New York, held back only by police barricades, to see their singing idol Tony Bennett. Today the children and grandchildren of those fans are enjoying the same experience. Perhaps what sums up Tony's legacy and longevity best was the observation The New York Times made in a review of "MTV Unplugged": "What accounts for the Bennett magic? Artistry certainly. The repertory is indeed classic…. But perhaps more important is his ability to convey a sense of joy, of utter satisfaction, in what he is doing."

Tony Bennett turned 80 on August 3, 2006, an event which has generated a wide range of tributes and celebrations. In addition to the release of **Duets – An American Classic**, RPM Records/Columbia Records/Legacy Recordings is launching a monumental and definitive reissue project, The Tony Bennett Master Series. Executive produced by Tony Bennett and Danny Bennett, the first five releases in The Tony Bennett Master Series include expanded editions of three Grammy winning titles—*I Left My Heart In San Francisco* (1962), *Perfectly Frank* (1992), and *MTV Unplugged* (1994)—as well as two brand-new 16-song collections: *Tony Bennett's Greatest Hits of the '50s* and *Tony Bennett's Greatest Hits of the '60s.*

A major television special, "Tony Bennett: An American Classic," is set to air on NBC television in November 2006.

Conceived and directed by Rob Marshall, executive produced by Danny Bennett, John DeLuca and Rob Marshall, produced by Jodi Hurwitz, "Tony Bennett: An American Classic"

will feature musical guests Elton John, Michael Bublé, John Legend, k.d. lang, Diana Krall, Christina Aguilera, Stevie Wonder, Barbra Streisand, Chris Botti, and Juanes. Segment hosts for the program include Robert DeNiro, Bruce Willis, Billy Crystal, Catherine Zeta-Jones and John Travolta.

Notables from the worlds of music, stage, screen and politics were on-hand to help Tony celebrate his 80th birthday at a star-studded party at the Museum of Natural History in New York. The evening included heartfelt tributes from Harry Belafonte, Bruce Willis, Katie Couric and former President Bill Clinton.

"As you know, I've always admired your singing and your ability to bring millions of people together across the generations through your music," said Clinton, who sent along taped greetings when he was unable to personally attend Bennett's birthday festivity due to a prior commitment.

"But you haven't stopped at your musical success. You've spent so much time working to bring people together through public service. I'll never forget your special performance at my First Inaugural, and I can't thank you enough for the support of the Clinton Global Initiative, even auctioning off one of your beautiful paintings for an enormous amount of money that will help to keep children around the world alive. I've valued our friendship so much over the years.

"You're still young, your ear is still pitch-perfect, you've got a light in your eye, and I hope this special day is just the beginning of many, many more happy birthdays to a very good man."

"Everything's all happening at once," said Bennett. "It's the biggest amount of recognition I've ever received—almost like a payoff for all the years of traveling on the road."

As the world's most boyish octogenarian, a vital musical artist at the peak of his powers, Tony Bennett is living proof that fairy tales can indeed come true when you're young at heart.

tonybennett.net

benedettoarts.com

columbiarecords.com

BECAUSE OF YOU

(duet with k.d. lang)

Words and Music by
Arthur Hammerstein and Dudley Wilkinson
Arranged by Dan Coates

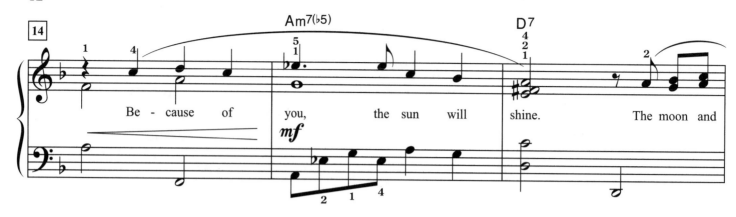

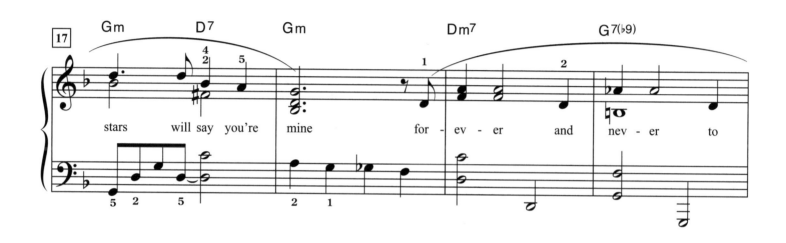

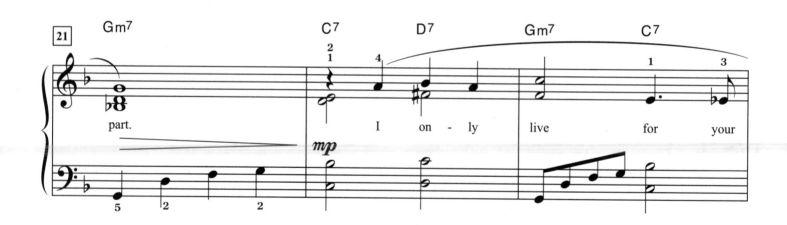

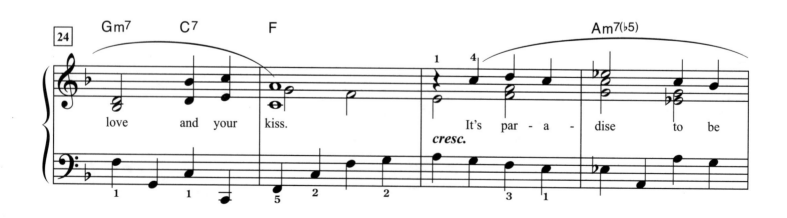

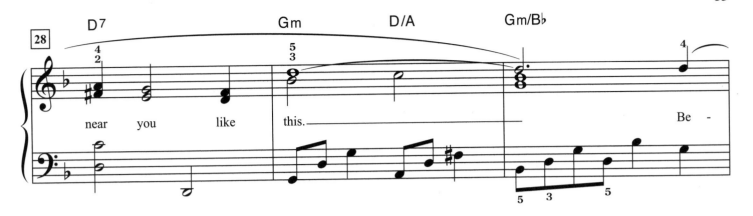

near you like this._____ Be -

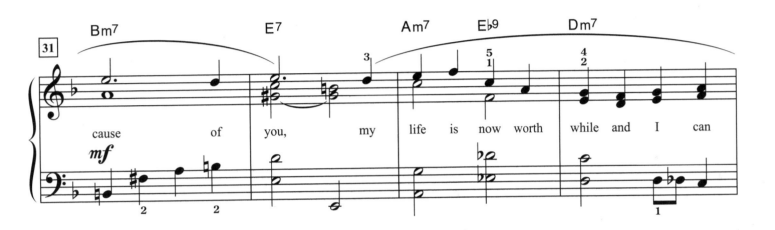

cause of you, my life is now worth while and I can

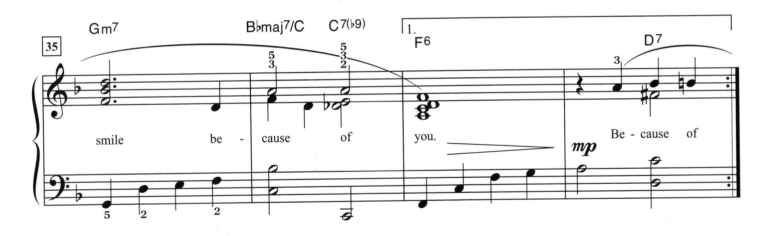

smile be - cause of you. Be - cause of

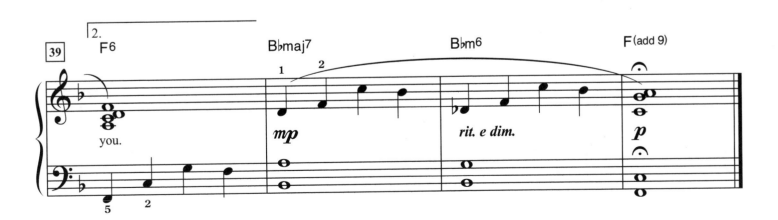

you.

ARE YOU HAVIN' ANY FUN?

(duet with Elvis Costello)

Music by Sammy Fain
Words by Jack Yellen
Arranged by Dan Coates

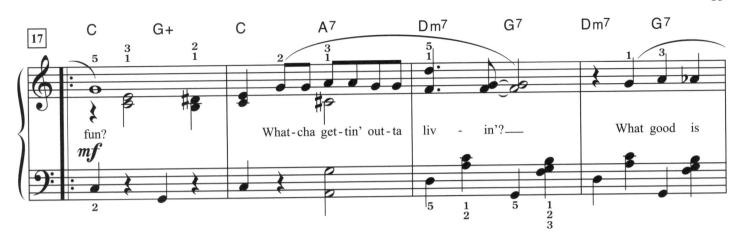

fun? What-cha get-tin' out-ta liv - in'?___ What good is

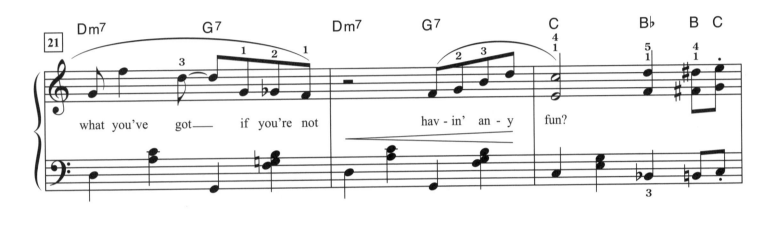

what you've got___ if you're not hav - in' an - y fun?

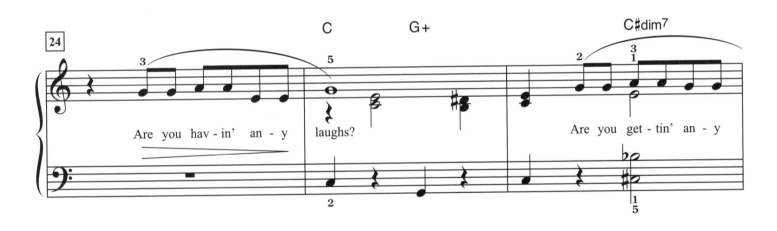

Are you hav - in' an - y laughs? Are you get-tin' an - y

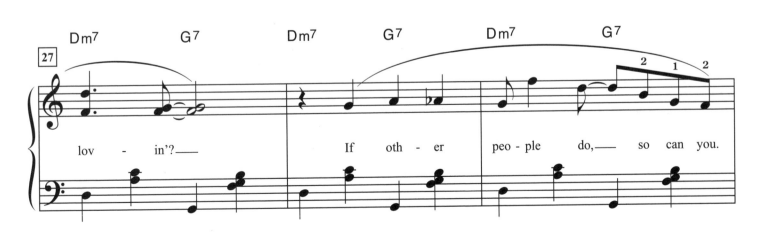

lov - in'?___ If oth - er peo - ple do,___ so can you.

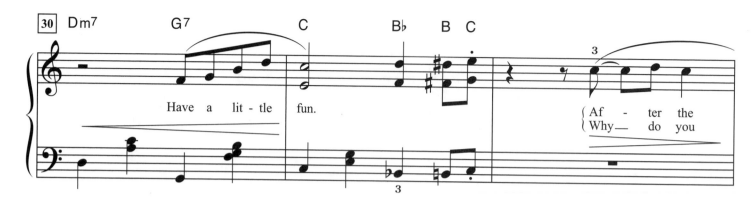

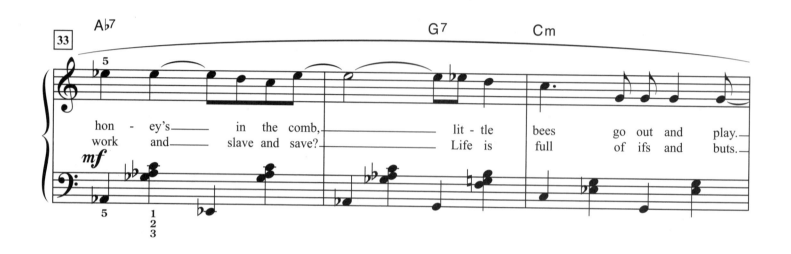

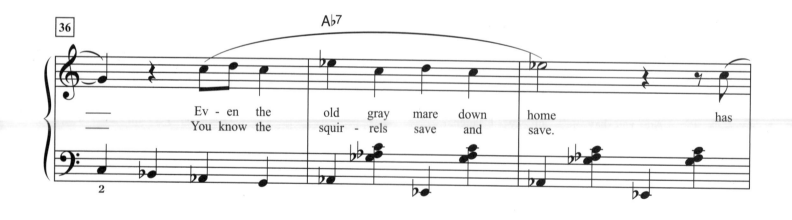

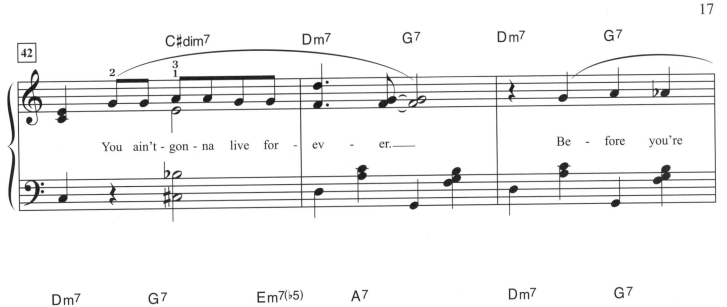

You ain't - gon - na live for - ev - er. ___ Be - fore you're

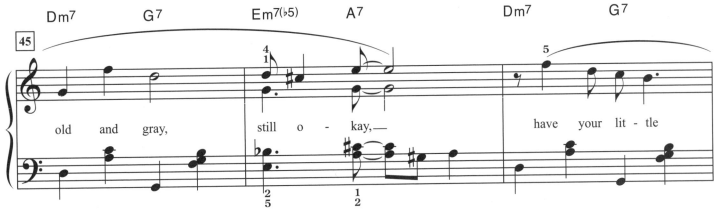

old and gray, still o - kay, ___ have your lit - tle

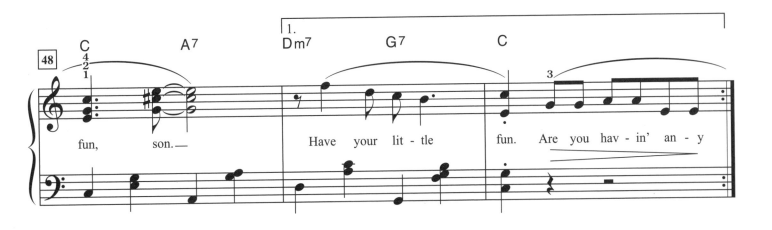

fun, son. ___ Have your lit - tle fun. Are you hav - in' an - y

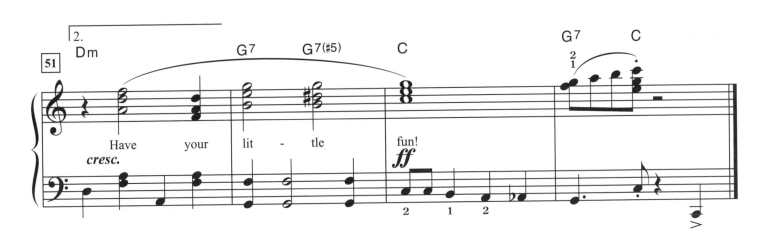

Have your lit - tle fun!

THE BEST IS YET TO COME

(duet with Diana Krall)

Music by Cy Coleman
Lyric by Carolyn Leigh
Arranged by Dan Coates

Out of the tree of life— I just picked me a plum,

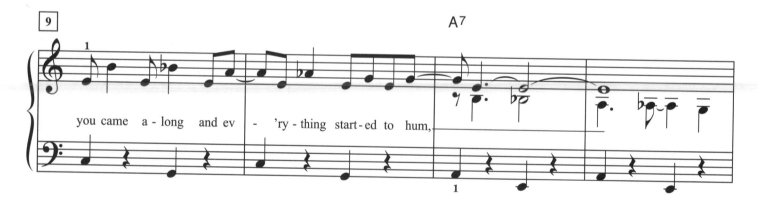

you came a-long and ev - 'ry-thing start-ed to hum,

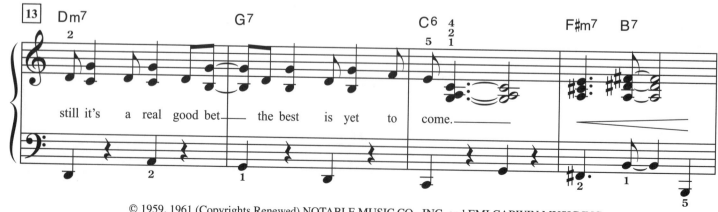

still it's a real good bet— the best is yet to come.—

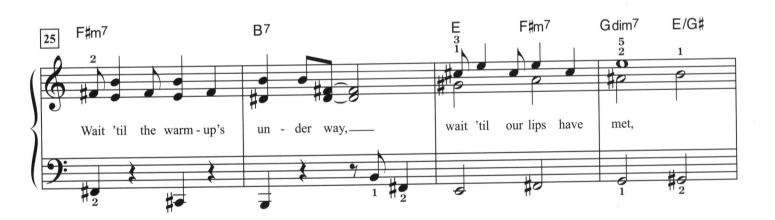

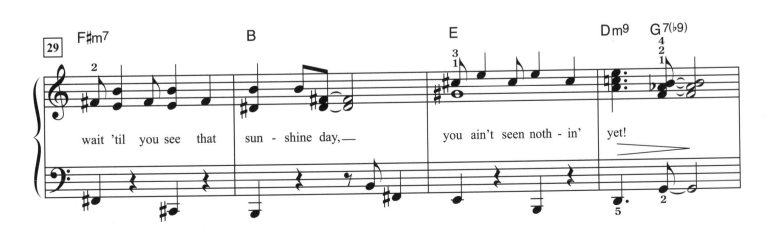

33 C ... A7

The best is yet to come— and, babe, won't that be fine,

mp

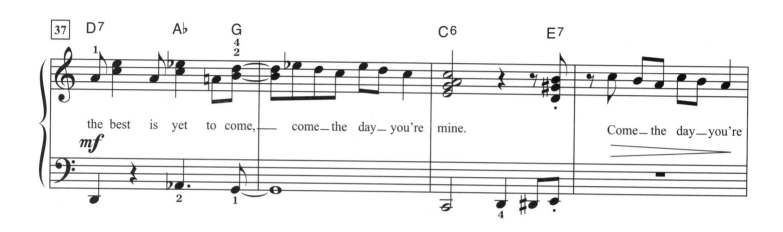

37 D7 ... Ab ... G ... C6 ... E7

the best is yet to come,— come— the day— you're mine. Come— the day— you're

mf

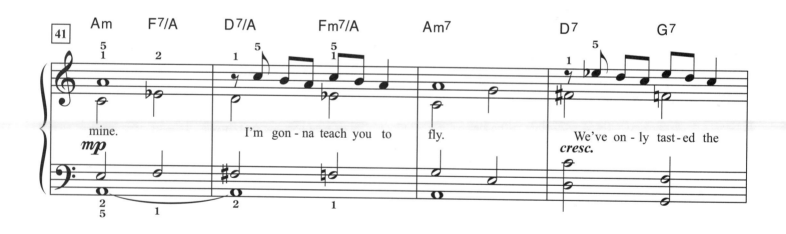

41 Am ... F7/A ... D7/A ... Fm7/A ... Am7 ... D7 ... G7

mine. I'm gon-na teach you to fly. We've on-ly tast-ed the

mp *cresc.*

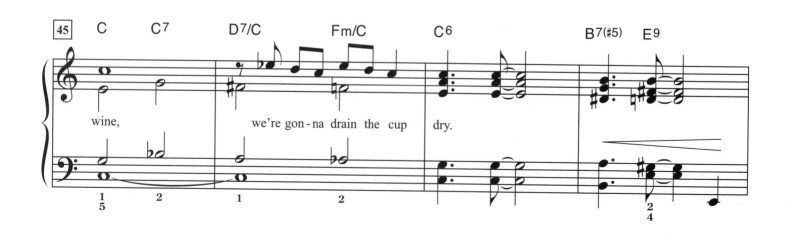

45 C ... C7 ... D7/C ... Fm/C ... C6 ... B7(#5) ... E9

wine, we're gon-na drain the cup dry.

Wait 'til your charms are ripe___ for these arms to sur - round.___

You think you've flown be - fore,___ but you ain't left the ground.___

Wait 'til you're locked in my em - brace,___

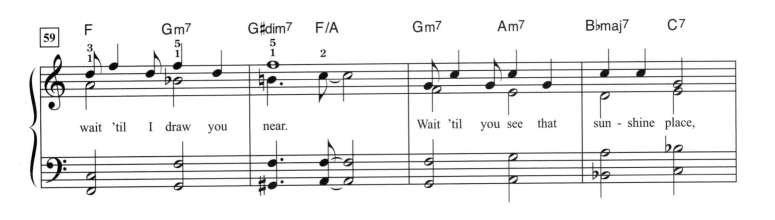

wait 'til I draw you near. Wait 'til you see that sun - shine place,

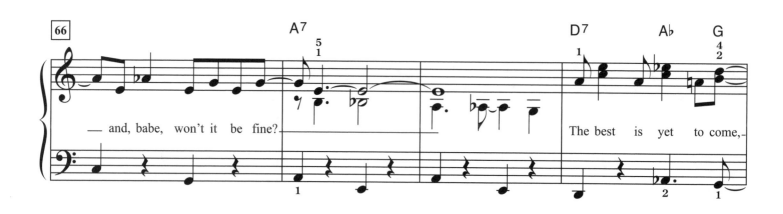

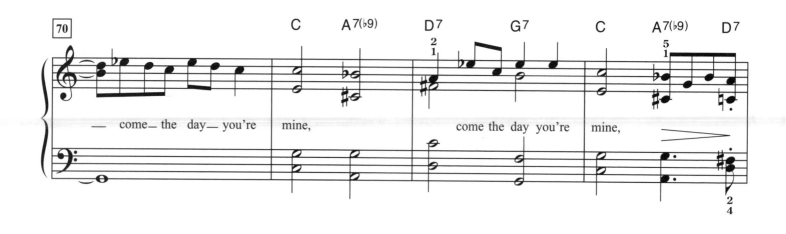

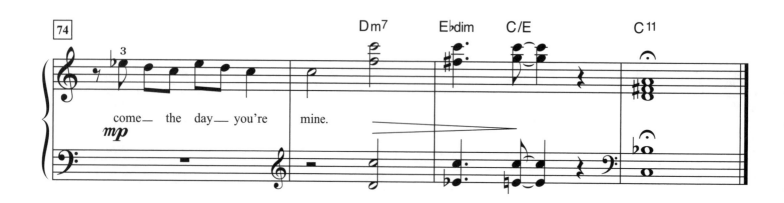

THE BOULEVARD OF BROKEN DREAMS

(duet with Sting)

Words by Al Dubin
Music by Harry Warren
Arranged by Dan Coates

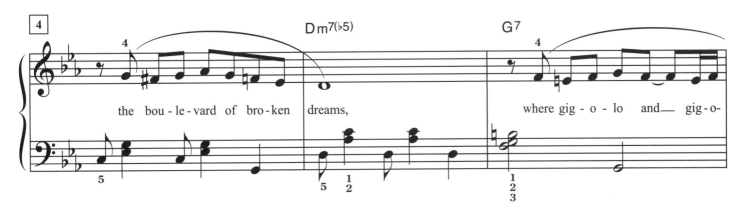

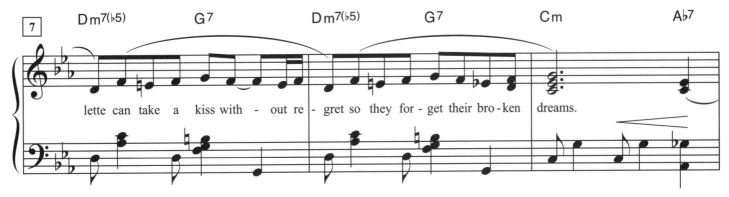

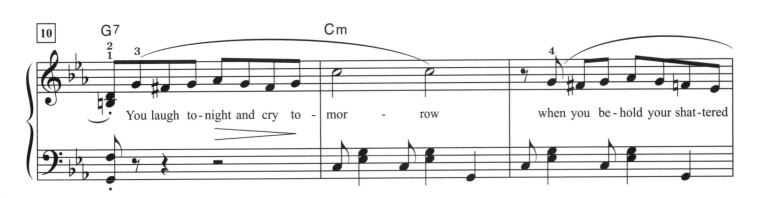

24

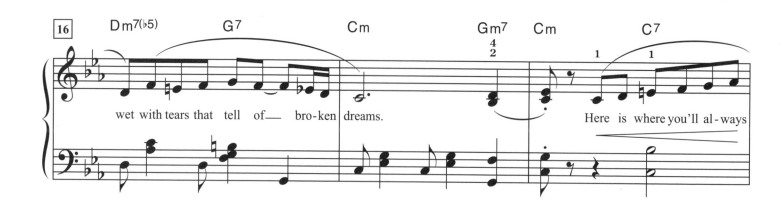

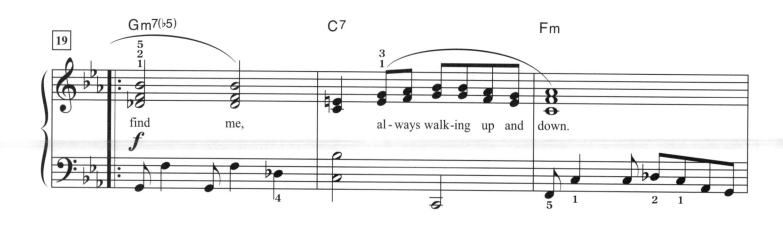

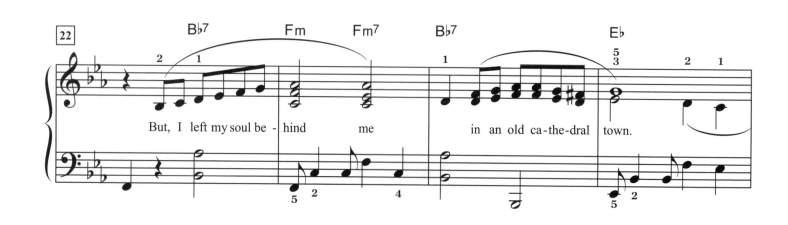

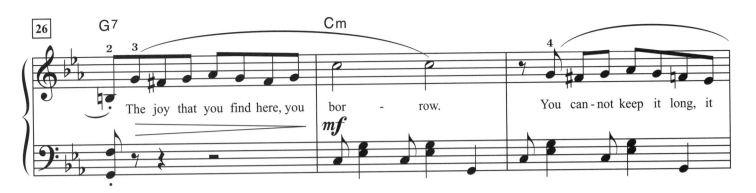

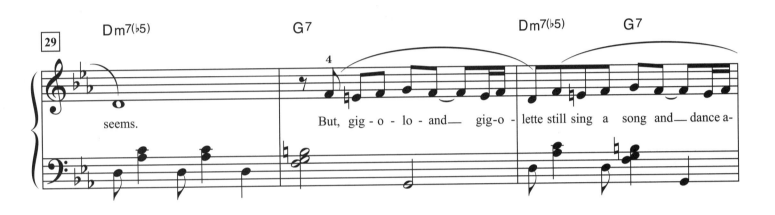

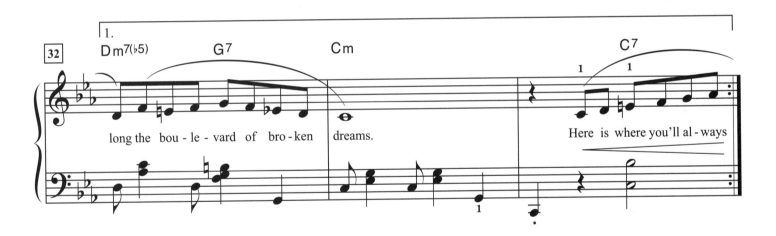

COLD, COLD HEART

(duet with Tim McGraw)

Words and Music by Hank Williams
Arranged by Dan Coates

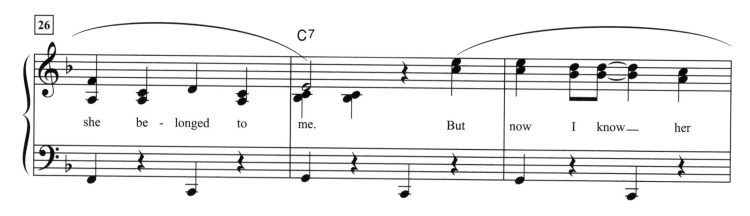

she be - longed to me. But now I know— her

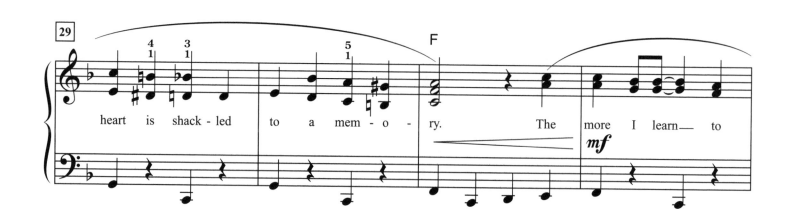

heart is shack - led to a mem - o - ry. The more I learn— to

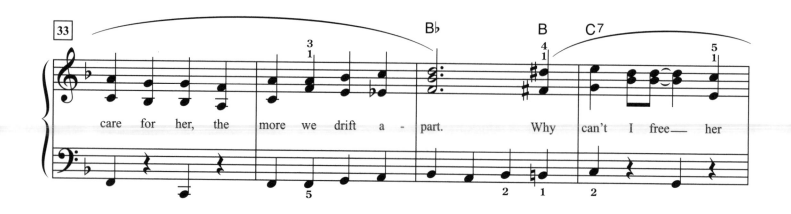

care for her, the more we drift a - part. Why can't I free— her

doubt - ful mind and melt her cold, cold heart.

FOR ONCE IN MY LIFE

(duet with Stevie Wonder)

Music by Orlando Murden
Lyrics by Ronald Miller
Arranged by Dan Coates

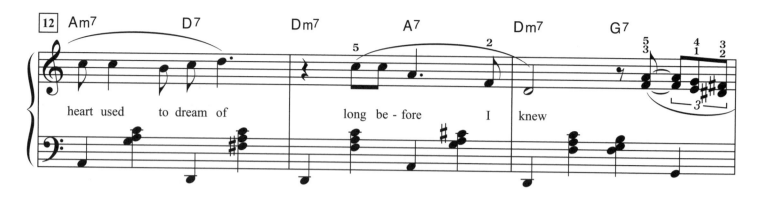

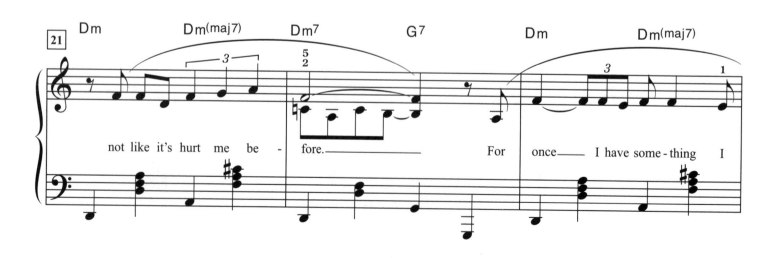

know won't de - sert me.   I'm— not a - lone   an - y - more.   For

once— I can say— this is   mine,— you can't take it.   Long— as I know— I have

cresc. poco a poco

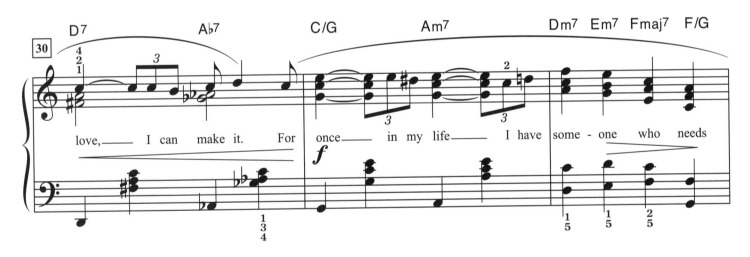

love,— I can   make it. For   once—— in my life—— I have some - one   who   needs

f

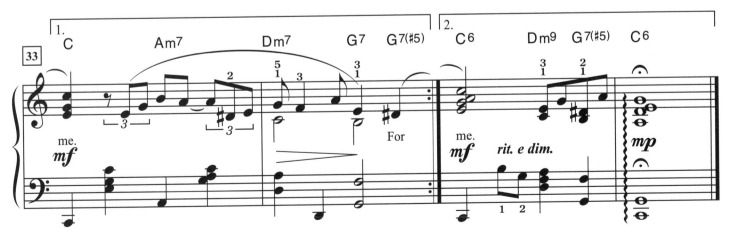

me.   For   me.

mf   mf   rit. e dim.   mp

THE GOOD LIFE

(duet with Billy Joel)

Words by Jack Reardon
Music by Sacha Distel
Arranged by Dan Coates

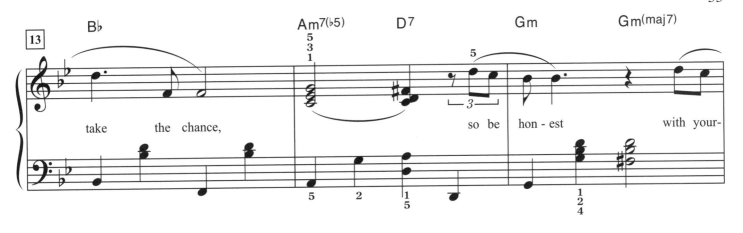

take the chance, so be hon - est with your-

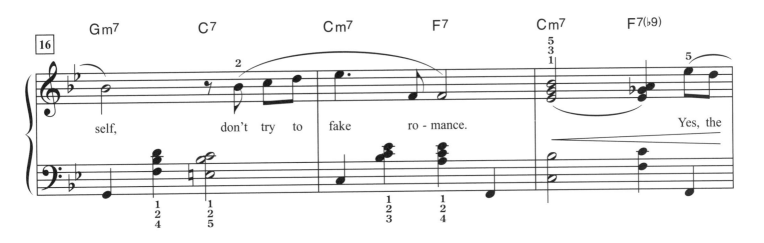

self, don't try to fake ro - mance. Yes, the

good life, to be free and ex - plore the un - known,

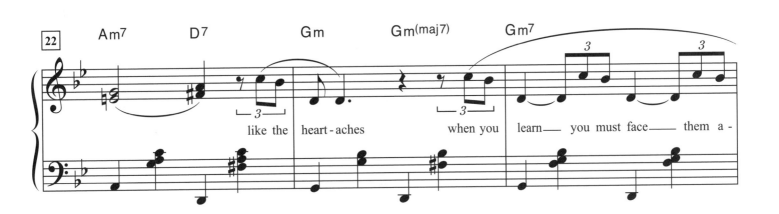

like the heart - aches when you learn you must face them a -

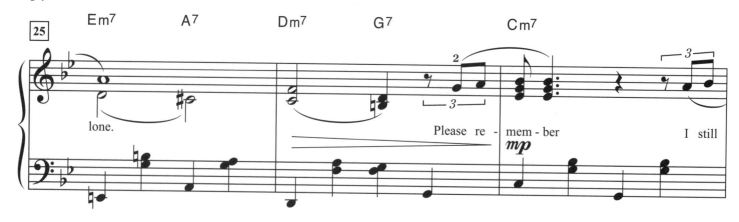

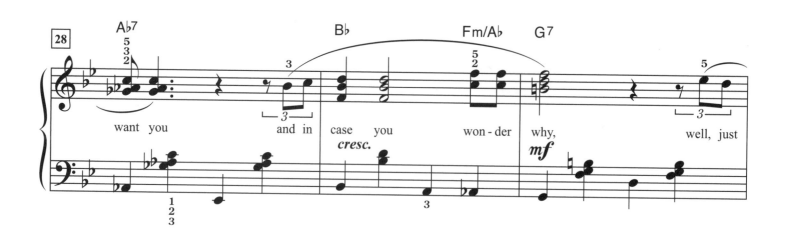

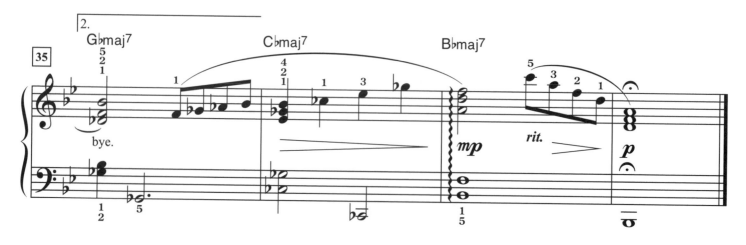

I LEFT MY HEART IN SAN FRANCISCO

Words by Douglass Cross
Music by George Cory
Arranged by Dan Coates

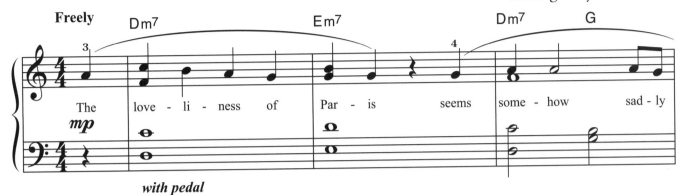

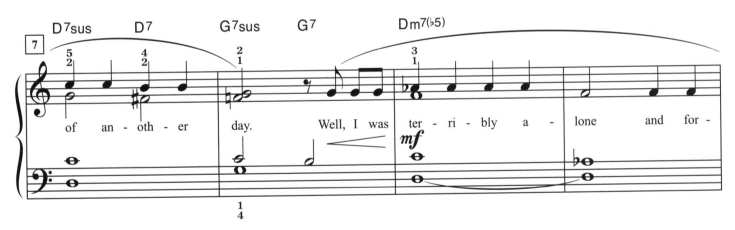

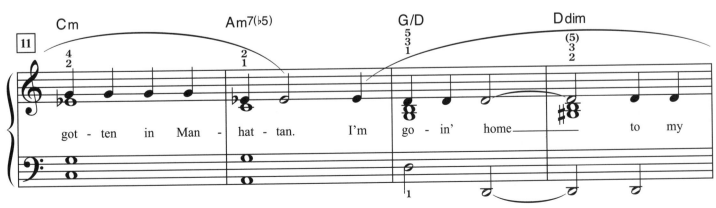

HOW DO YOU KEEP THE MUSIC PLAYING?

(duet with George Michael)

Lyrics by Alan and Marilyn Bergman
Music by Michel Legrand
Arranged by Dan Coates

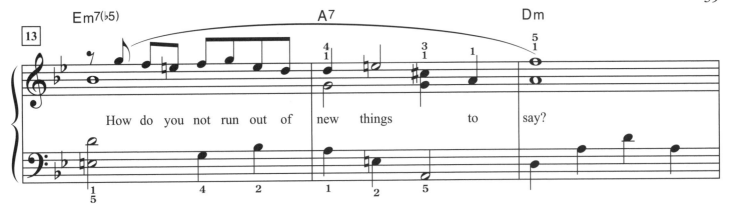

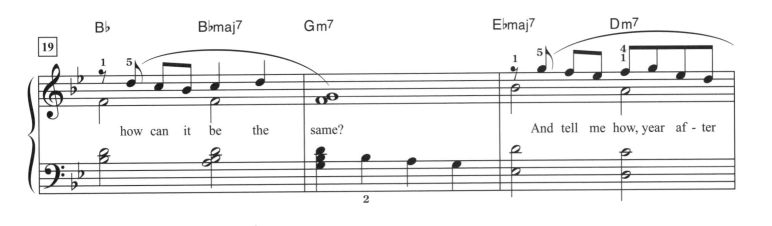

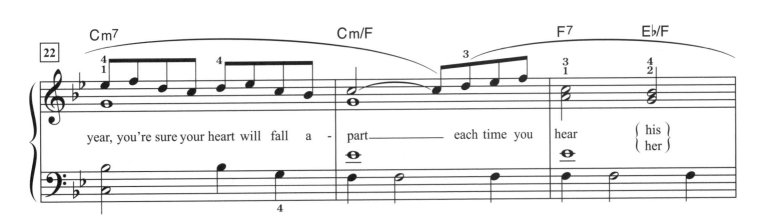

40

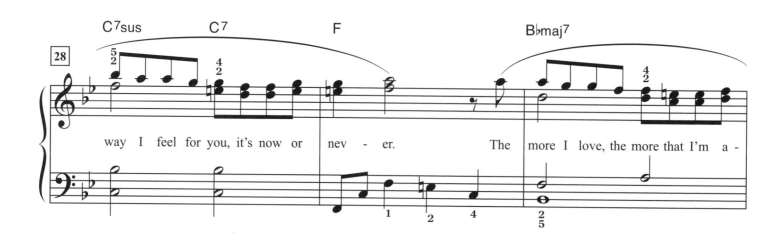

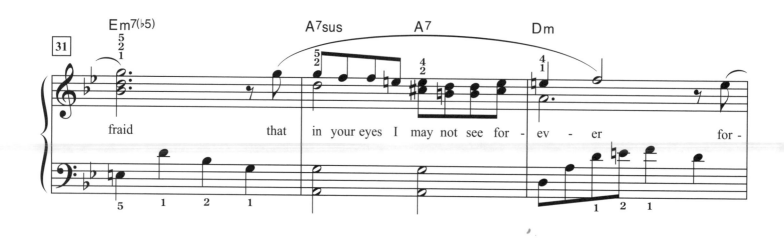

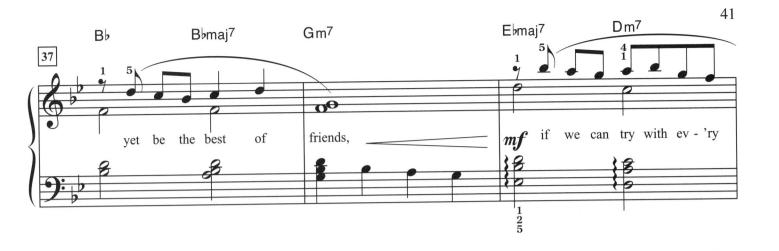

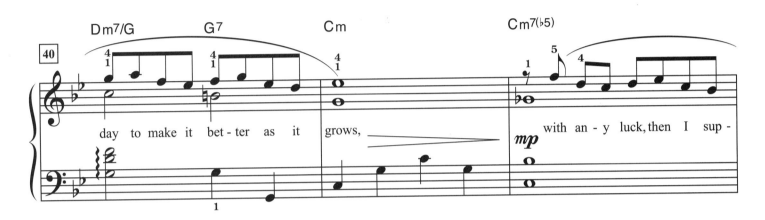

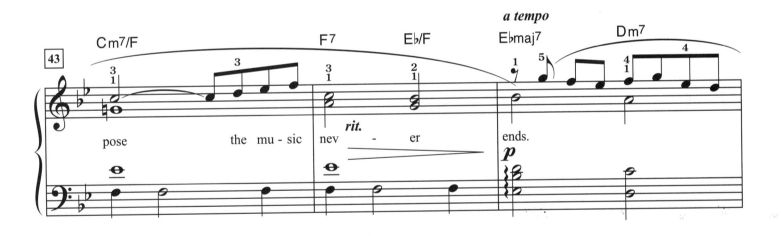

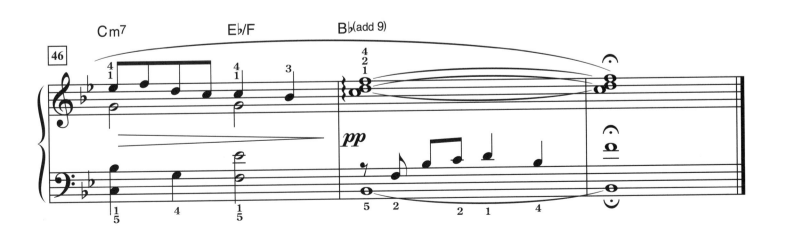

I WANNA BE AROUND

(duet with Bono)

Words and Music by
Johnny Mercer and Sadie Vimmerstedt
Arranged by Dan Coates

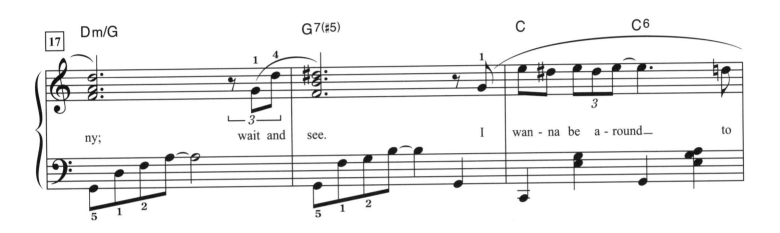

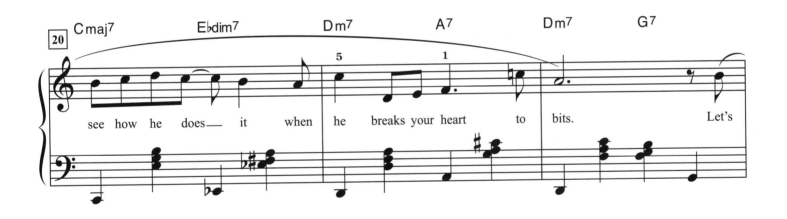

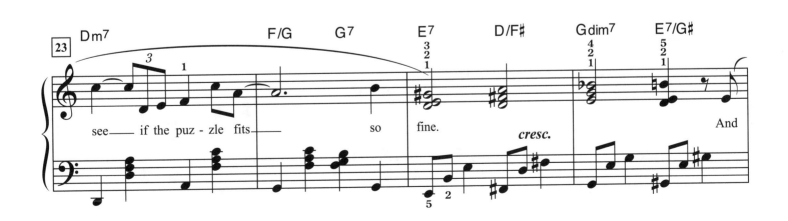

that's when I'll dis - cov - er that re - venge is sweet___ as I sit there ap - plaud-ing from a

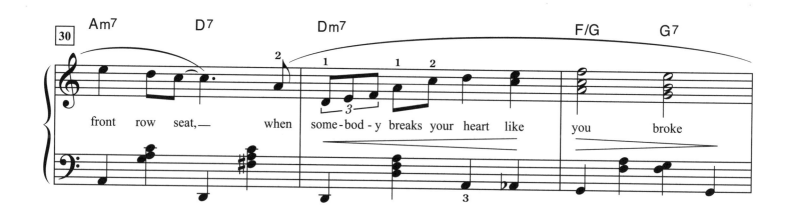

front row seat,___ when some-bod - y breaks your heart like you broke

mine. I mine.

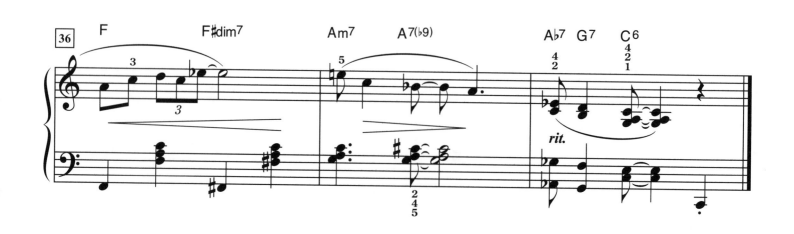

IF I RULED THE WORLD

(duet with Celine Dion)

Music by Cyril Ornadel
Words by Leslie Bricusse
Arranged by Dan Coates

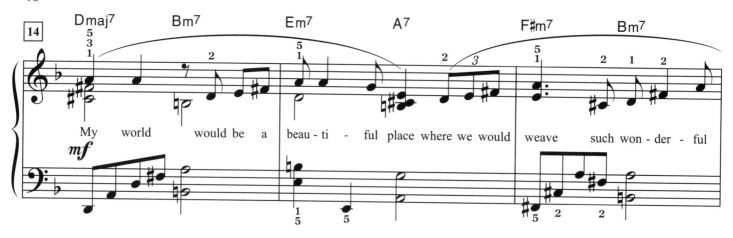

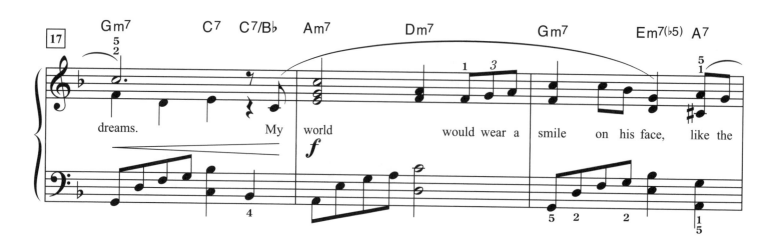

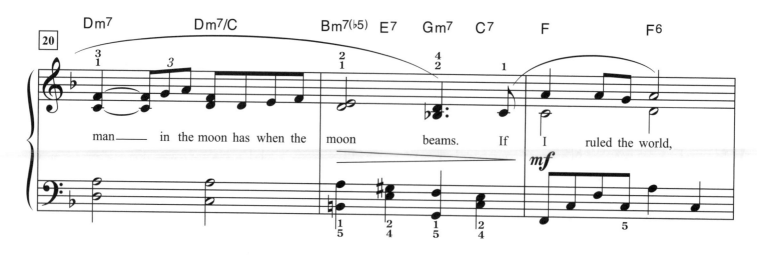

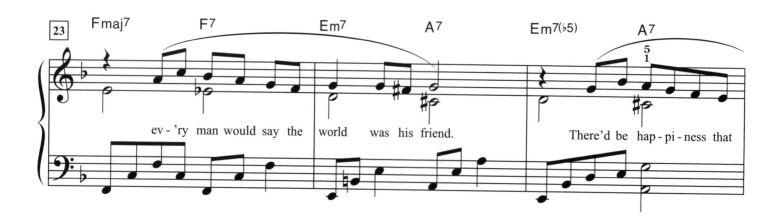

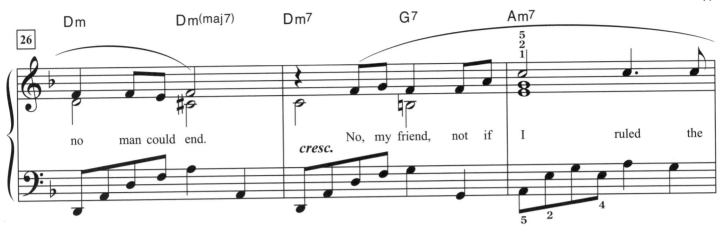

no man could end.   No, my friend, not if I ruled the

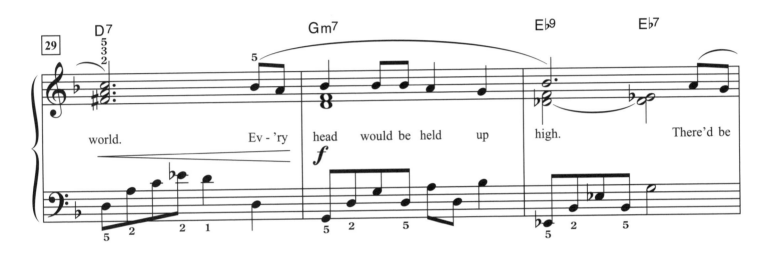

world.   Ev - 'ry head would be held up high.   There'd be

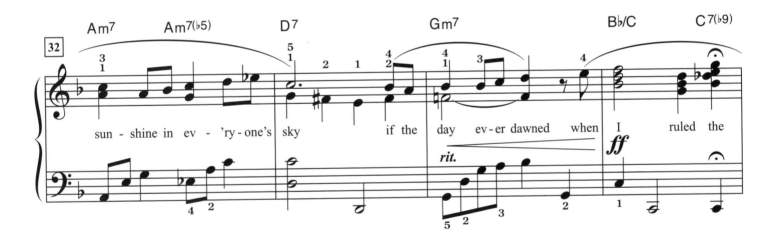

sun - shine in ev - 'ry-one's sky   if the day ev - er dawned when I ruled the

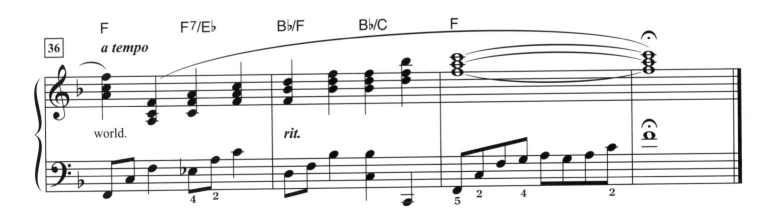

world.

JUST IN TIME

(duet with Michael Bublé)

Lyrics by Betty Comden and Adolph Green
Music by Jule Styne
Arranged by Dan Coates

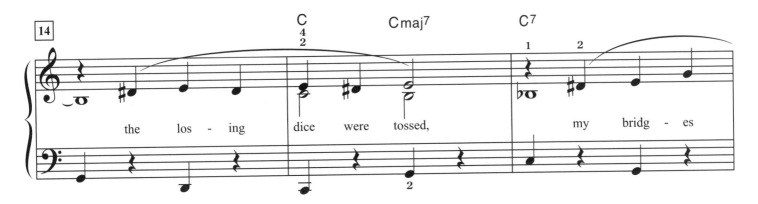

the los - ing dice were tossed, my bridg - es

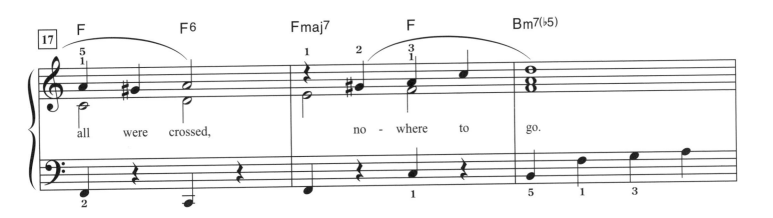

all were crossed, no - where to go.

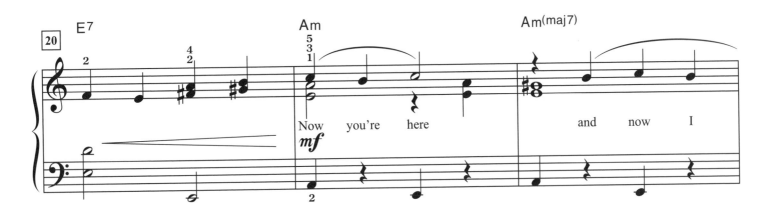

Now you're here and now I

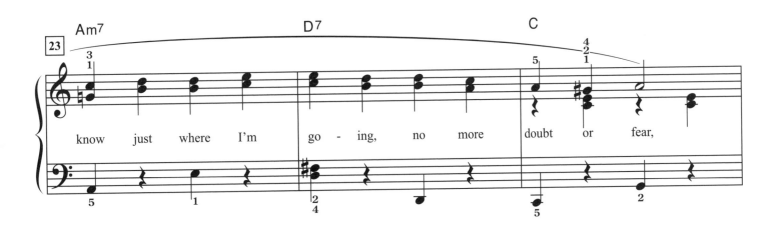

know just where I'm go - ing, no more doubt or fear,

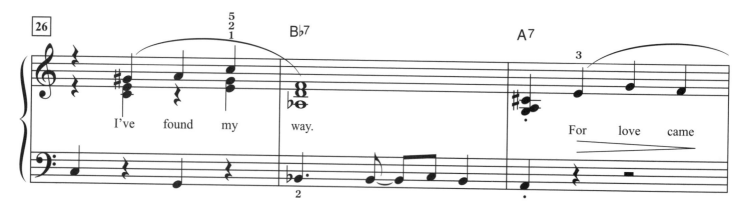

I've found my way. For love came

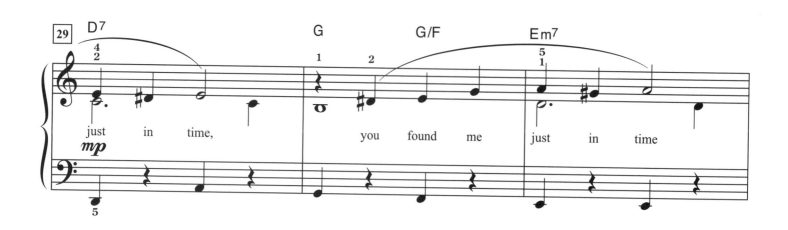

just in time, you found me just in time

and changed my lone - ly life that love - ly

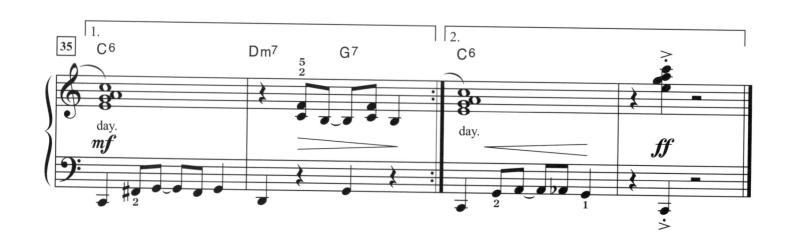

day. day.

LULLABY OF BROADWAY

(duet with the Dixie Chicks)

Words by Al Dubin
Music by Harry Warren
Arranged by Dan Coates

PUT ON A HAPPY FACE

(duet with James Taylor)

Music by Charles Strouse
Lyric by Lee Adams
Arranged by Dan Coates

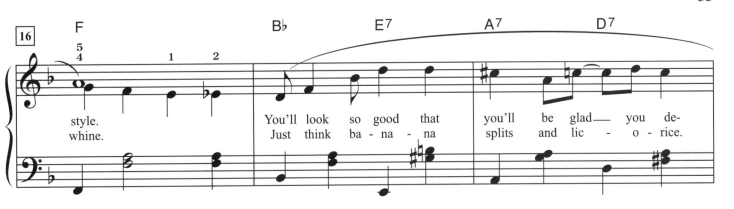

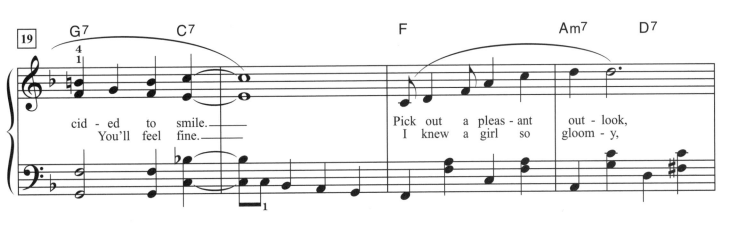

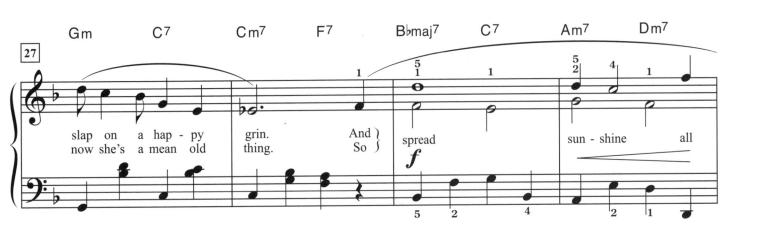

56

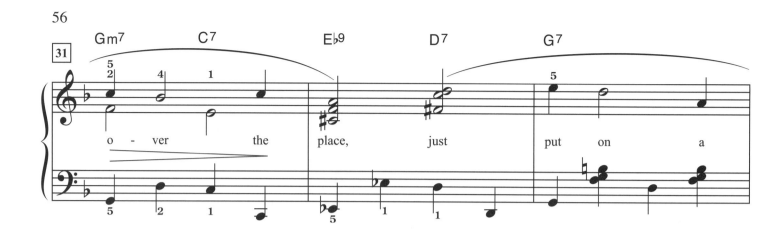

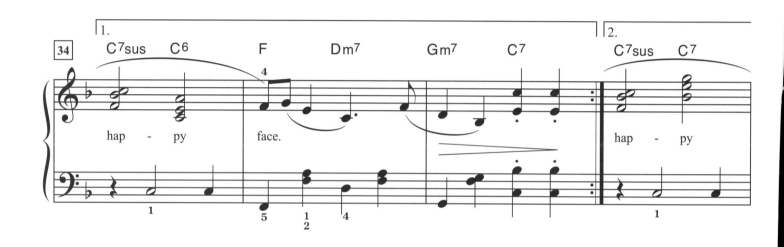

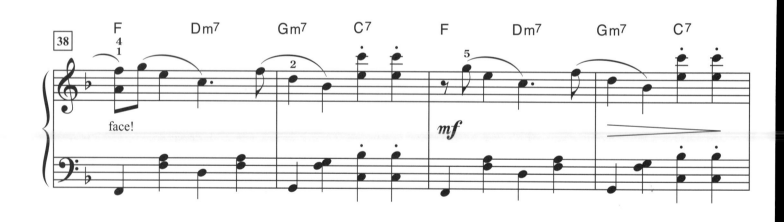

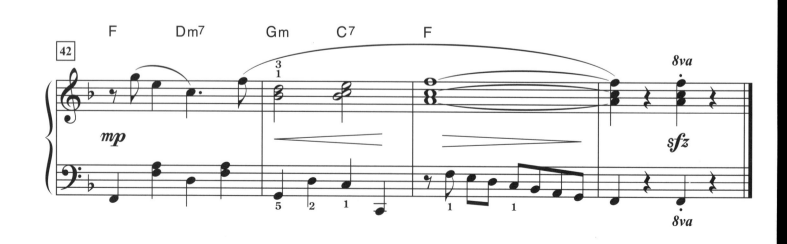

THE SHADOW OF YOUR SMILE

(duet with Juanes)

Music by Johnny Mandel
Lyric by Paul Francis Webster
Arranged by Dan Coates

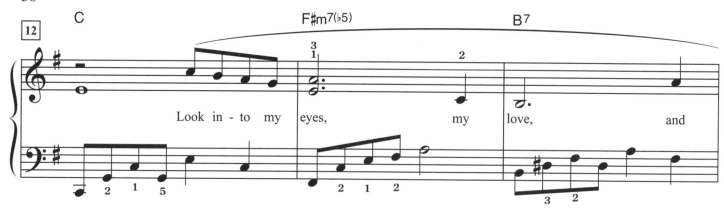

Look in - to my eyes, my love, and

see all the love - ly things you

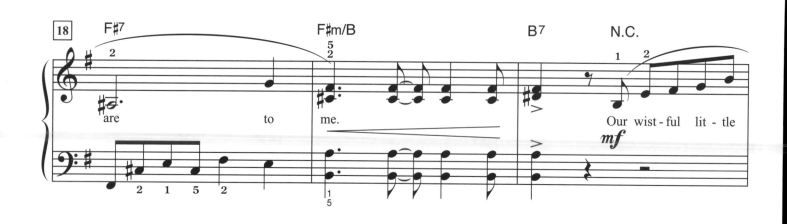

are to me. Our wist - ful lit - tle

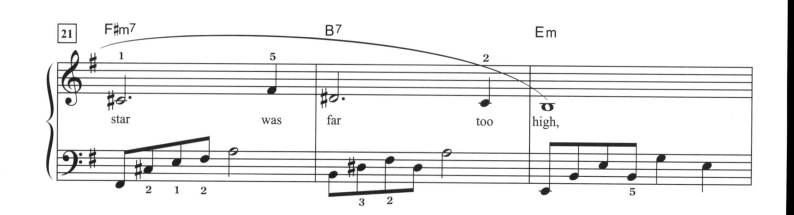

star was far too high,

RAGS TO RICHES

(duet with Elton John)

Words and Music by
Richard Adler and Jerry Ross
Arranged by Dan Coates

SING, YOU SINNERS

(duet with John Legend)

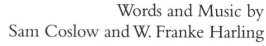

Words and Music by
Sam Coslow and W. Franke Harling
Arranged by Dan Coates

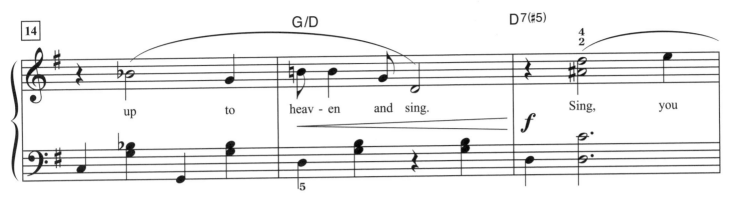

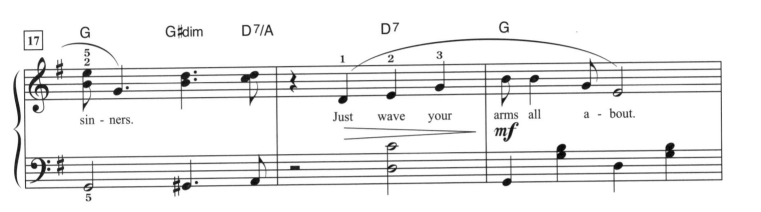

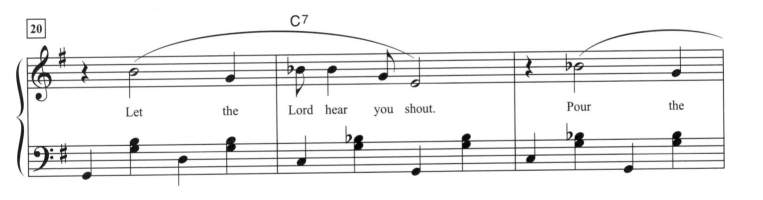

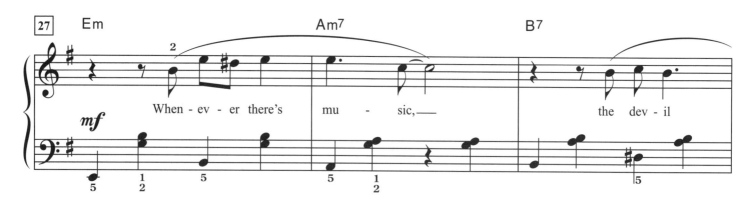

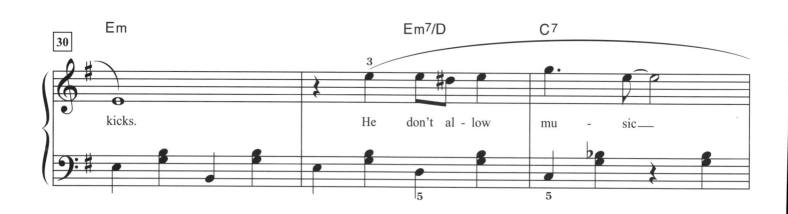

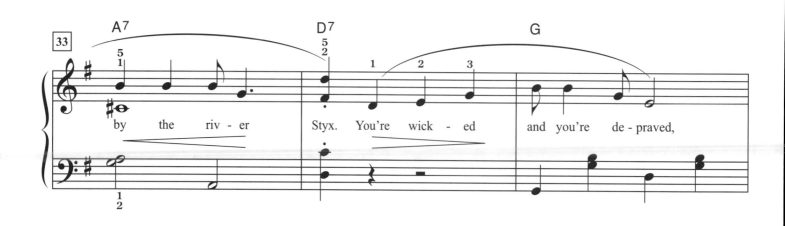

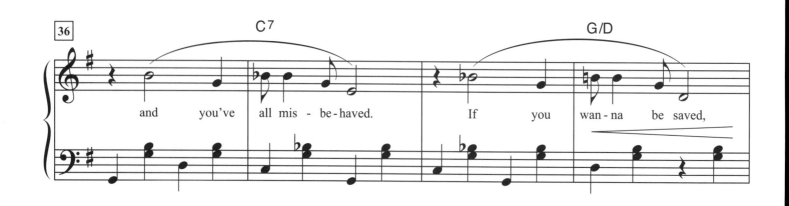

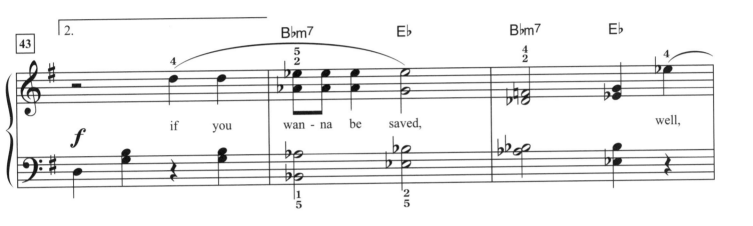

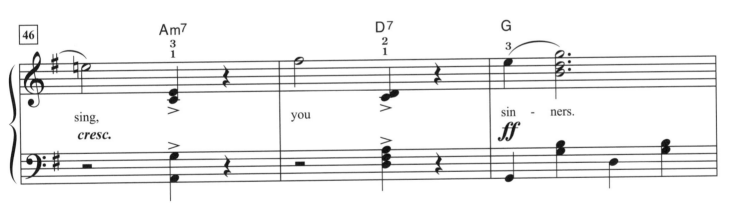

SMILE

(duet with Barbra Streisand)

Words by John Turner and Geoffrey Parsons
Music by Charles Chaplin

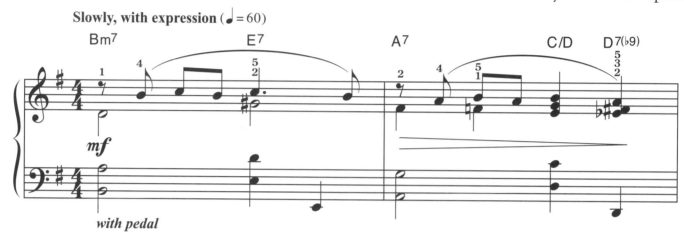

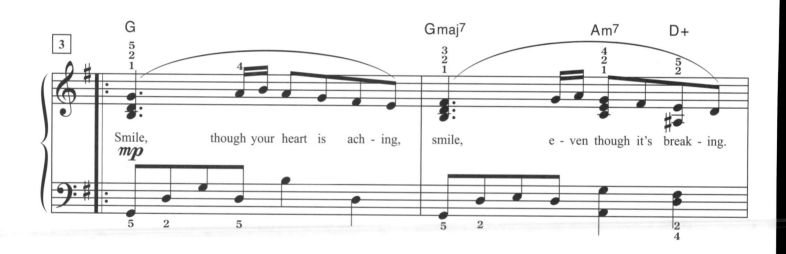

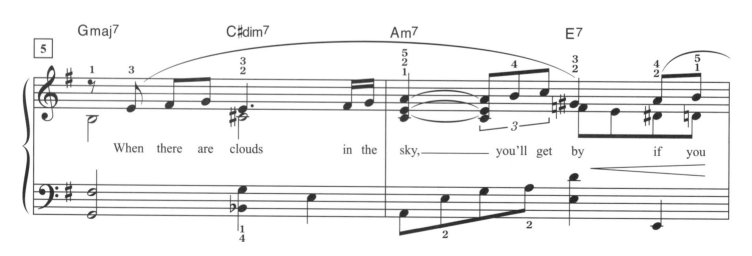

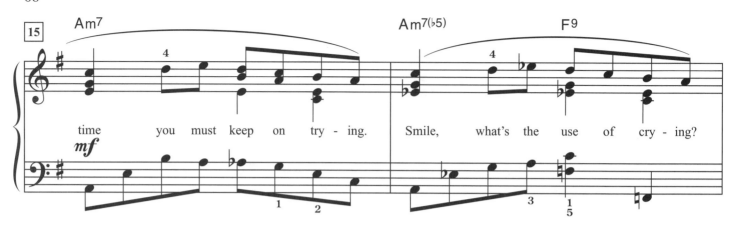

time　you must keep on　try - ing.　Smile,　what's the use of cry - ing?

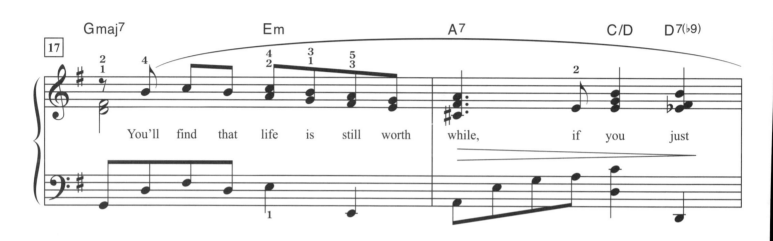

You'll find that life is still worth while, if you just

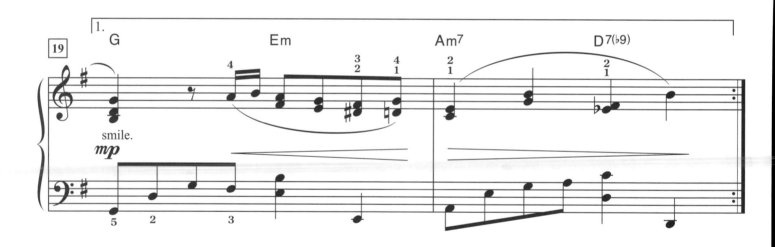

smile.

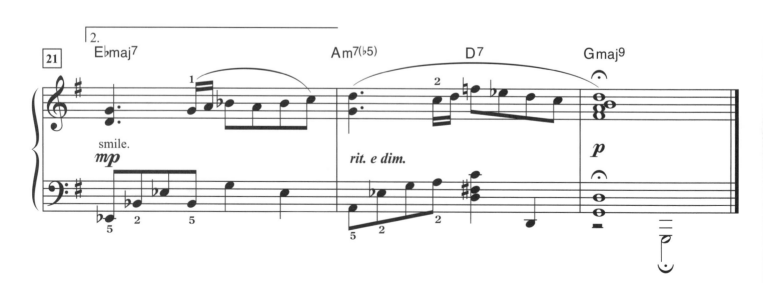

smile.

rit. e dim.

THE VERY THOUGHT OF YOU

(duet with Paul McCartney)

Words and Music by Ray Noble
Arranged by Dan Coates

70

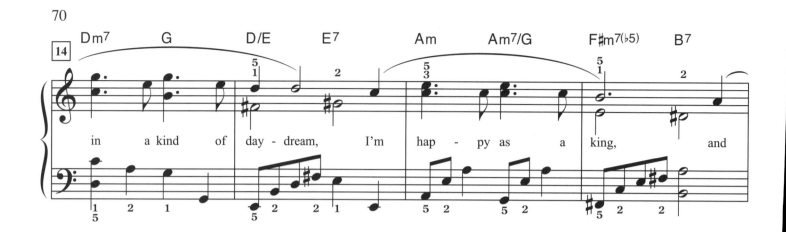

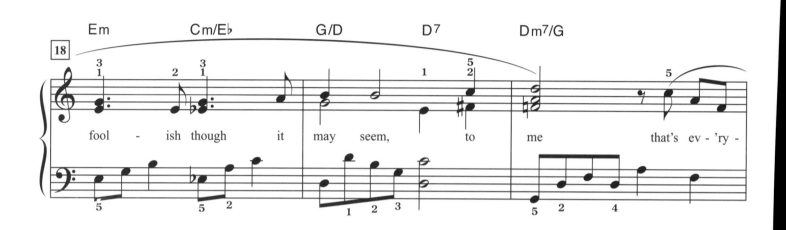

mo - ments go till I'm near to you. I see your

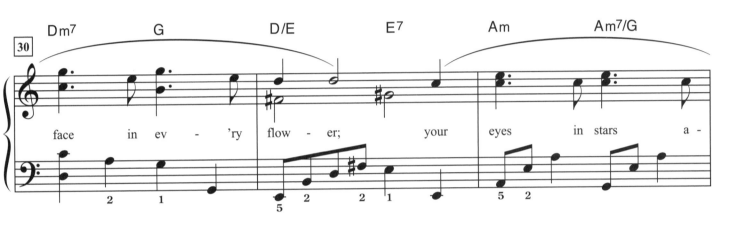

face in ev - 'ry flow - er; your eyes in stars a -

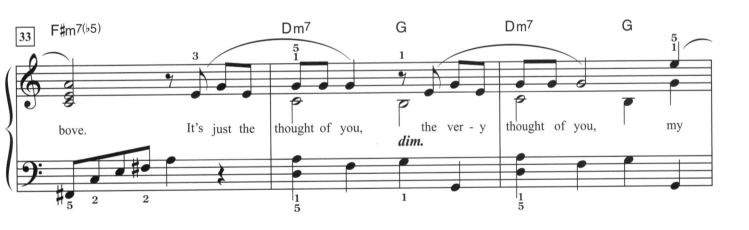

bove. It's just the thought of you, the ver - y thought of you, my

love. The ver - y love.